Kids' Travel Guide
Spain

FlyingKids Presents:

Kids' Travel Guide

Spain

Author: Wendy Crawford and Shiela H. Leon

Editor: Carma Graber
Graphic designer: Neboysha Dolovacki
Cover Illustrations and design: Francesca Guido
Published by FlyingKids Limited

Visit us @ www.theflyingkids.com

Contact us: leonardo@theflyingkids.com

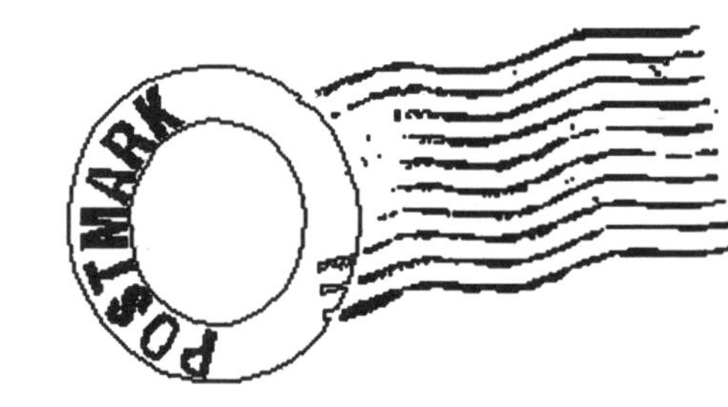

ISBN: 978-1-910994-12-2

Acknowledgement:

All images are from Adobe Stock except those listed below:

Graphic Stock: 10bgl, 18bg, 27bg, 28-all images, 29-all images, 31mc, 31mr, 35mb; Shutterstock: 11m, 14; Unsplash: 29m1, 29m4, 35m1, 35m2.

Attribution: 19t-By MatthiasKabel, CC-BY-SA-3.0, via Wikimedia Commons, 36t-By Emilio J. Rodríguez-Posada (Museo del Prado 2016) [CC BY-SA 2.0, via Wikimedia Commons, 36c-By Museoreinasofia (Own work), via Wikimedia Commons, 36c-By PA (Own work) CC BY-SA 4.0, via Wikimedia Commons.

Key: t=top; b=bottom; l=left; r=right; c=center; m=main image; bg=background

Table of Contents

This is the only page for parents in this book ...

Dear Parents,

If you bought this book, you're probably planning a family trip with your kids. You are spending a lot of time and money in the hopes that this family vacation will be pleasant and fun. You would like your children to learn a little about the country you visit—its geography, history, unique culture, traditions, and more. And you hope they will always remember the trip as a very special experience.

The reality is often quite different. Parents find themselves frustrated as they struggle to convince their kids to join a tour or visit a landmark, while the kids just want to stay in and watch TV. On the road, the children are glued to their mobile devices instead of enjoying the new sights and scenery—or they complain and constantly ask, "When are we going to get there?" Many parents are disappointed after they return home and discover that their kids don't remember much about the trip and the new things they learned.

That's exactly why *Kids' Travel Guide—Spain* was created.

How does it work?

A family trip is fun. But difficulties can arise when children are not in their natural environment. *Kids' Travel Guide—Spain* takes this into account and supports children as they get ready for the trip, visit new places, learn new things, and finally, return home.

Kids' Travel Guide—Spain does this by helping children to prepare for the trip and know what to expect. During the trip, kids will read relevant facts about Spain and get advice on how to adapt to new situations. The kids will meet Leonardo—their tour guide. Leonardo encourages them to experiment, explore, and be more involved in the family's activities—as well as to learn new information and make memories throughout the trip.

Kids' Travel Guide—Spain includes puzzles, tasks to complete, useful tips, and other recommendations along the way. In addition, kids are asked to document and write about their experiences during the trip, so that when you return home, they will have a memoir that will be fun to look at and reread again and again.

Kids' Travel Guide—Spain offers general information about Spain, so it is useful regardless of the city or part of the country you plan to visit. It includes basic geography; flag, symbols, and coins; basic history; and colorful facts about culture and customs in Spain.

Ready for a new experience?

Have a nice trip and have fun!

Hi, Kids!

If you are reading this book, it means you are lucky – you are going to **Spain**!

You probably already know what areas you will visit, and you may have noticed that **your parents** are getting ready for the journey. They have bought **travel guides**, looked for information on the **Internet**, and **printed pages** of information. They are talking to friends and people who have already visited **Spain**, in order to learn about it and know what to do, where to go, and when … But this is not just another **guidebook** for your parents.

THIS BOOK IS FOR YOU ONLY – THE YOUNG TRAVELER.

So what is this book all about?

First and foremost, meet **Leonardo**, your very own personal guide on this trip. **Leonardo** has visited many places around the **world** (guess how he got there 😉), and he will be with you throughout the **book** and the **trip**.

Leonardo will tell you all **about** the **places** you will visit – it is always good to learn a little bit about the country and its history beforehand. He will provide many **ideas**, **quizzes**, **tips**, and **other surprises**.

Leonardo will accompany you while you are packing and leaving home. He will stay in the **hotel** with you (don't worry, it does not cost more money 😉)! And he will see the sights with you until you **return home**.

A Travel Diary – The Beginning!

Going to Spain!!!

By plane / ship / car / other ______________

We will stay in Spain for __________ days.

Is this your first visit ? yes / no

Where will you sleep? In a hotel / In a hostal / In a campsite /

In an apartment / With family / Other ______________

What places are you planning to visit?

____

____

____

What special activities are you planning to do?

____

____

____

Are you excited about the trip?

This is an excitement indicator. Ask your family members how excited they are (from "not at all" up to "very, very much"), and mark each of their answers on the indicator. Leonardo has already marked the level of his excitement …

not at all — very, very much

Leonardo

Who is traveling?

Write down the names of the family members traveling with you and their answers to the questions.

Paste a picture of your family.

Name: ____________

Age: ______

Have you visited Spain before? yes / no

What is the most exciting thing about your upcoming trip?

____

____

____

Name: ____________

Age: ______

Have you visited Spain before? yes / no

What is the most exciting thing about your upcoming trip?

____

____

____

Name: ____________

Age: ______

Have you visited Spain before? yes / no

What is the most exciting thing about your upcoming trip?

____

____

____

Name: ____________

Age: ______

Have you visited Spain before? yes / no

What is the most exciting thing about your upcoming trip?

____

____

____

Name: ____________

Age: ______

Have you visited Spain before? yes / no

What is the most exciting thing about your upcoming trip?

____

____

____

Preparations at home – DO NOT FORGET ...!

Mom or Dad will take care of packing clothes (how many pairs of pants, which comb to take ...). Leonardo will only tell you the stuff he thinks you might want to bring along on your trip to Spain.

Leonardo made a Packing List for you. Check off each item as you pack it!

- ☐ *Kids' Travel Guide – **Spain*** – of course
- ☐ Comfortable walking shoes
- ☐ A raincoat or umbrella (Sometimes it rains without warning.)
- ☐ A hat (and sunglasses, if you want)
- ☐ Pens and pencils
- ☐ Crayons and markers (It is always nice to color and paint.)
- ☐ A notebook or writing pad (You can use it for games or writing, or to draw or doodle in when you're bored ...)
- ☐ A book to read
- ☐ Your smartphone/tablet or camera

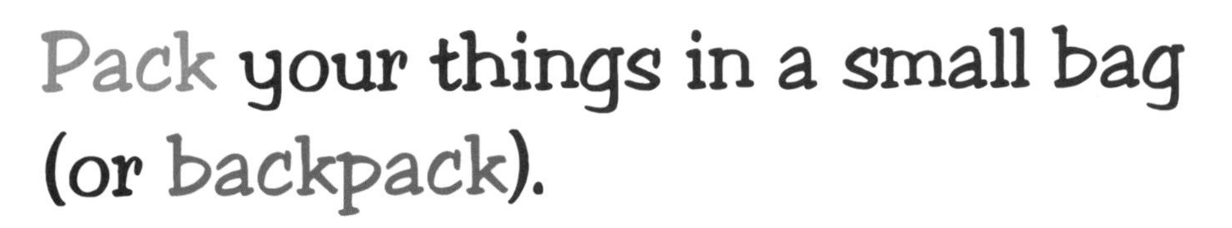

Pack your things in a small bag (or backpack).

You may also want to take these things:

Snacks, fruit, candy, and chewing gum. If you are flying, chewing gum can help a lot during takeoff and landing, when there's pressure in your ears.

Games you can play while sitting down: electronic games, booklets of crossword puzzles, connect-the-numbers (or connect-the-dots), etc.

Remember to take a notebook or a writing pad. You can use it for games, writing, or to draw or doodle in when you are bored …

Now let's see if you can find 12 items you should take on a trip in this word search puzzle:

- ☐ Leonardo
- ☐ walking shoes
- ☐ hat
- ☐ raincoat
- ☐ crayons
- ☐ book
- ☐ pencil
- ☐ camera
- ☐ snacks
- ☐ fruit
- ☐ patience
- ☐ good mood

P	A	T	I	E	N	C	E	A	W	F	G
E	L	R	T	S	G	Y	J	W	A	T	O
Q	E	Y	U	Y	K	Z	K	M	L	W	O
H	O	S	N	A	S	N	Y	S	K	G	D
A	N	R	Z	C	P	E	N	C	I	L	M
C	A	M	E	R	A	A	W	G	N	E	O
R	R	A	I	N	C	O	A	T	G	Q	O
Y	D	S	G	I	R	K	Z	K	S	H	D
S	O	A	C	O	A	E	T	K	H	A	T
F	R	U	I	T	Y	Q	O	V	O	D	A
B	O	O	K	F	O	H	Z	K	E	R	T
T	K	Z	K	A	N	S	I	E	S	Y	U
O	V	I	E	S	S	N	A	C	K	S	P

Welcome to Spain!

Welcome to magical España!!

That's the Spanish word for Spain. Spain is the sunniest country in Europe. And with over 60 million visitors a year, it is the third most popular destination in the world!

Quizzes! Can you guess which countries get more visitors?

Answer: France and the United States

Do you think you'll be like most visitors and fall in love with Spain during the first five minutes you're here? Leonardo hopes so. That's why he wants to share some of the things he loves the most about Spain—its history and many different cultures, plus the beautiful scenery and fun things to do.

There is at least one thing in Spain for everyone to fall in love with! You'll find almost 5,000 km (over 3,000 miles) of sunny coastlines. There are rugged cliffs and unexplored snowy mountains, deserts, 15 national parks, lively and historic cities, and a happy mix of many cultures.

No two Spanish cities are alike. Each has its own history and story to tell.

And the Spanish people are as interesting as their country. They love people, and they love to talk. They get so excited that **they use their hands** to help explain what they're saying. When you meet someone, you'll get a hug and a kiss on each cheek.

The hardest part about visiting Spain is figuring out which place you like the most!

Did you know?
Spain has a special festival called "La Tomatina." Thousands of people come every year to the town of Buñol to throw tomatoes ***(tomate)*** at each other and have a party!

Bay of Biscay

Santander

Oviedo

French Republi

Vitoria-Gasteiz

Spain on the map

Spain is on the continent of Europe. It is one of the two countries that make up the Iberian Peninsula. Portugal is the other country.

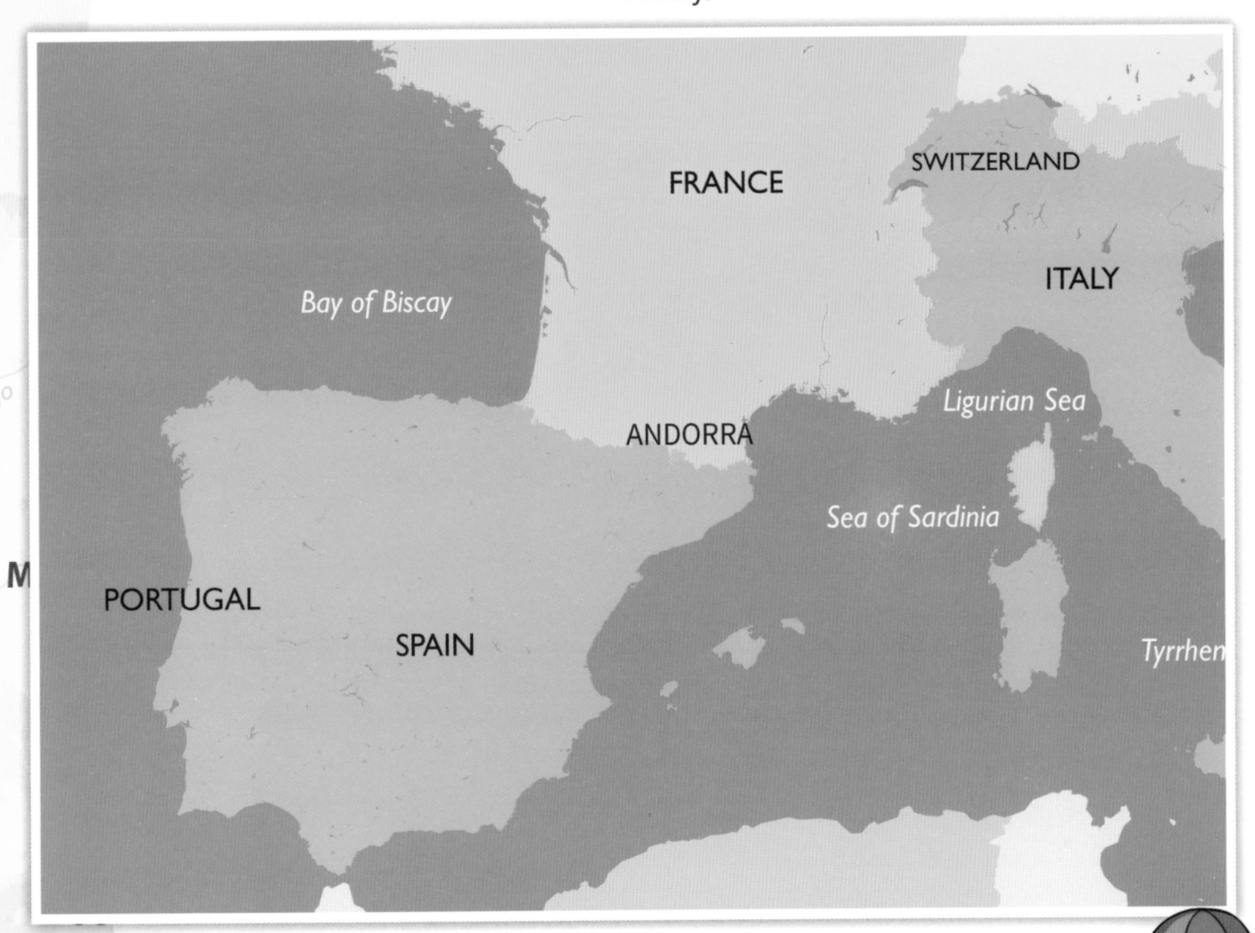

Did you know?
Spain is the second largest country in the European Union. The biggest country is France, one of Spain's neighbors.

Can you find France on the map?
Can you see a tiny country between Spain and France? What's the name of this country? ____________.

Answer: Andorra

Morocco

What is a compass rose?

A compass rose is a design that shows the directions:
North – South – East – West. Since North is always marked on maps, you can always figure out where the other directions are.
A compass rose is drawn on the face of a compass, and the hand always points North. When you know where each direction is, it is easier to figure out where you are … and how to get to where you want to be.

Write down the three missing directions in the blank squares.

North

Spain is surrounded by oceans, seas, and three countries. **Can you help Leonardo find them on the map?**

On the east, from Spain's top to bottom, is the ______________ Sea.

At the bottom of Spain is the ______________ Ocean.

On the west side of Spain is a country named ______________.

On Spain's northwest and north is the ______________ of ______________.

In Spain's northeast are the *Pyrenees* Mountains.

Can you name the country on the other side of the mountains?

____

Answers: Mediterranean Sea; Atlantic Ocean; Portugal; Bay of Biscay; Pyrenees Mountains; France.

All about borders

In order to separate countries, borders were invented.
Sometimes, a border is part of the natural landscape—like a river, a mountain range, or an ocean.
Other times a border is man-made. It might be shown by lines drawn on a map, or maybe by a fence, a wall, or a sign.
All of Spain's borders are **natural borders except for its border with Portugal**.
That border was made in 1297—almost a thousand years ago!!!!
The provinces of Spain (like the provinces in Canada or the states in Australia and the United States) also have borders, but people can cross them at any time. There are no fences or walls; there is usually just a sign along the road.

Did you know?
The border between Spain and Portugal is the longest unbroken border in Europe. It is 1,214 kilometers (or 754 miles) long.

Quizzes!

Spain has islands! Do you know what their names are? (A hint: you can check the map on the previous page.)

Answers: The Balearic Islands and the Canary Islands.

You are about to visit beautiful Spain. Can you find 10 Spanish cities in the search puzzle?

- ☐ Madrid
- ☐ Seville
- ☐ Barcelona
- ☐ Granada
- ☐ Bilbao
- ☐ Valencia
- ☐ Cordoba
- ☐ Segovia
- ☐ Malaga
- ☐ Toledo

B	E	M	T	R	P	A	O	B	K
M	D	L	V	F	B	D	A	N	B
L	A	G	L	O	G	R	L	D	I
G	L	D	D	I	C	T	T	A	L
V	Q	R	R	E	V	L	C	D	B
W	O	M	L	I	J	E	Z	A	A
C	T	O	L	E	D	O	S	N	O
J	N	A	I	C	N	E	L	A	V
A	S	E	G	O	V	I	A	R	W
A	G	A	L	A	M	V	F	G	C

Let's have a look at Spain's main cities ...

Madrid—the capital

Welcome to Madrid—the capital city of Spain!

What is the capital of your country? ____________

In the center of Madrid, there is the big and important plaza called **Puerta del Sol**. This means "Gate of the Sun."

Puerta del Sol is the place where all the people come when something important is happening. If you want to pronounce the name like a real Spaniard, say it like this: pwerta del sol.

Puerta del Sol and **Plaza Mayor** are the heart of Old Town Madrid. This is the very first part of Madrid that was built. The plazas are really big, and the streets are very narrow because in old times, horses didn't take up as much room as cars do now.

There are many other historical places in Old Madrid: **Palacio Real** (Royal Palace), the art museum **El Prado**, the large and beautiful park called **Retiro Parque**, and the lively public squares **Plaza Santa Ana** and **Plaza Cibeles.**

Did you know?
Madrid has a special symbol: It is the statue of a bear and a strawberry tree. It is called **El Oso y El Madrono**.

Can you guess where to find the famous statue?
Hint: It is in the most important square in Madrid.

Beautiful Barcelona!

Barcelona is one of the most beautiful and elegant cities in Europe …
Many of Spain's greatest artists lived in Barcelona—including Pablo Picasso, Jean Miró, and Salvador Dali.

Have you heard of them?

Never | I've heard the name | I know who they are

Did you know?
Barcelona was always a busy Mediterranean port city, but it never had any beaches … until 25 years ago.

How is that possible?
Before the 1992 Olympic Games in Barcelona, there were only big ugly buildings along the coast. They were used to store shipping stuff for the port. No one wanted to see that! So the city designed man-made beaches to make the area look good for the Olympics.

Have you heard about Gaudí?
Gaudí was a Spanish architect and artist who didn't like straight lines. This is why you can find many buildings that look different from any you have ever seen.

The most famous Gaudí building is the **Sagrada Família Basilica**. They started to build it in 1882, and it is still not completed.
Can you figure out how many years it has taken so far?

____

Las Ramblas is the heart of Barcelona's old quarter (called the Gothic Quarter). It is made of up five major avenues.

Can you guess which of these buildings was designed by Gaudí?

Seville—completely different

Seville is completely different from Madrid and Barcelona. That's because it has a different history and climate. In Seville, the summers are very, **very hot** and sunny. The temperature is often over 38 degrees Celsius (100 degrees Fahrenheit). But the good news is that in the winter, it doesn't get very cold.

Long ago, Seville and the whole region of Andalucía was ruled by **the Moors** (Muslims from North Africa). At that time, Seville was the center of education and culture for **all of Europe**.

Seville's Old Town is where the city first began. It has many famous churches, monuments, and historical places.

The **Seville Cathedral** is the **second** largest church in the world!

La Giralda, the cathedral's bell tower, was built In 1184 as the minaret* for the original mosque.

You can climb to the top by walking up 35 ramps that are wide enough for **two horses** walking side by side!

*A minaret is the tall, slender tower of a mosque with a balcony from which Muslims are called to prayer.

Did you know?
Christopher Columbus is buried in Seville. At least, they think so ...
Do you know what he did?

What does NO8DO mean?
You often see it on walls, buses, sidewalks, and sewer covers. That's because it's Seville's motto. It means "Seville has not abandoned me."

NO8DO

If you want to say it like a proud Sevillano, you should pronounce it like this: **"No me ha day-ha-doe."**

Answer: Discovered America in 1492.

This is the flag of Spain. The red and yellow represent the colors of Spain's original kingdoms.

Do you know what the symbol inside the flag is? It's called a coat of arms. Spain's coat of arms represents both the old kingdoms and modern Spain.

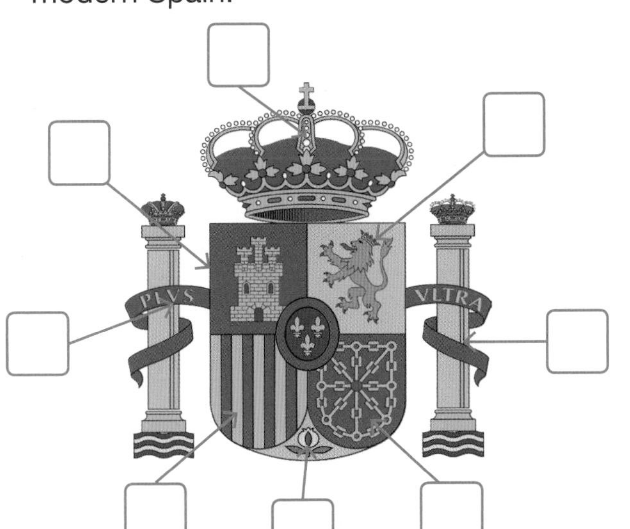

Do you know what each part of the coat of arms stands for?
Leonardo knows, but he forgot where each part is located. Can you help him by guessing the name of each part and putting its number in the right box?

1. Kingdom of León
2. Kingdom of Castile
3. Royal Crown of Spain's monarchy
4. Crown of Aragon
5. Kingdom of Navarre
6. Pillars of Hercules (Straits of Gibraltar)
7. Kingdom of Granada

Spain has another famous symbol—the Osborne Bull.
It is a very big silhouette of a brave black bull. You can find a statue of the bull sitting high on top of some hills. In the city, the bull is sometimes on top of a building. How many bulls did you see? ____________

Did you know?
In Spanish, the word for bull is toro. Practice saying toro. Leonardo will help you: tor-oh.

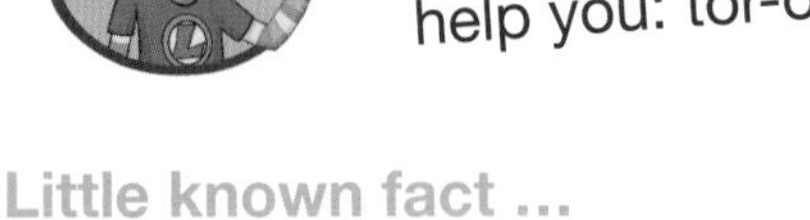

Little known fact ...
Spain's national anthem has **no words**! Everyone hums it! Only three other countries in the world have national anthems without words. Does your country's national anthem have words? If so, do you know them?

Paper money **and** coins ...

The type of money a country uses is called its "currency." Today Spain uses the euro—but it wasn't always so.

First came the silver **duro**, the **escudo**, and **reales**. Then in 1869, the **peseta** (pay-set-ta) replaced them. The peseta was the official currency for Spain until 2002.

Spain was an original member of the group of countries that formed the European Union (EU). When the EU issued the euro in 2002, Spain replaced the peseta with the Spanish euro.

This is the sign for the euro: **€**. Eleven of the EU countries use the **€** today.

In the EU there are eight different Spanish coins.

Spain's paper money has seven different bills. The bills come in 5, 10, 20, 50, 100, 200, and 500 € amounts.

Can you find coins with the picture of the king? How many €s are each worth? ______ ______

Answer: 1€ and 2€

EU countries can decorate their own coins, but the coins have the same value in all EU countries. You can spend a Spanish € in France, or be paid in Spain with an Italian €.

Every so often you can still see the old peseta notes and coins in use—so keep your eyes open for them. The peseta coin with the hole is the easiest one to spot.

Spain's long and exciting history

Spain is a very old country …

But HOW do we know that?
Early people lived in caves because they didn't have saws to cut wood or cement to build houses. One of the earliest caves ever used as a home is near Santander in Spain's north.

It is called the Cave of Altamira. It was used between **14,000 and 18,500** years ago! The early people painted pictures on the walls. This was their way of writing stories.

A **long** time later, around **3000 BC and 2000 BC** (BC: before Christ), two different tribes appeared in Spain. The Celts in the north and the Iberians in the south. The Celts were warlike—while the Iberians were more artistic and social.

Then in 1100 BC or so, the Phoenicians and Greeks settled along the coasts of southern and eastern Spain.

A thousand years later, in 100 BC, the Carthaginians and Romans invaded the Iberian Peninsula. They were enemies. Both wanted to control Spain, so they went to war.

The Romans finally won, and by 19 BC, all of Spain became part of the Roman Empire.

Leonardo is a little confused about all those different groups.
Can you help him by filling their names in the boxes …

14,000 to 18,500 years ago	3000 and 2000 BC	1100 BC	100 BC	19 BC
Cave of Altamira used by early humans.				

Answers (from left to right): Celts and Iberians; Phoenicians and Greeks; Carthaginians and Romans; Roman Empire.

Who came next?

The **Romans** ruled Spain for **700** years. They gave Spain some marvelous things, like watering systems for fields (**irrigation**) and **aqueducts** (channels), but over time, the Romans grew weak …

Visigoths (tribes from Germany) invaded the north of Spain in 400 AD (AD means after Christ was born). They stayed over 300 years, and they controlled parts of the Iberian peninsula … until the Moors arrived.

The **Moors** (Muslims from North Africa) invaded the south of Spain. By 718 AD they conquered a lot of Spain and forced the Visigoths out.

The capital of **Islamic Spain** was in **Andalucía**. In Arabic, it's called **Al-Andalus.**

Seville became the center of education, culture, trade, and scientific discoveries for all of Europe for almost 800 years.

These years are called **"The Golden Age of Spain."**

The word Moor is also used to mean Muslim and Islamic Spain.

Try to put the right invader in each time-box …

19 BC – 400 AD	400 AD	718 AD

Answers (from left to right): Romans; Visigoths; Moors.

And then what happened?

By the 1400s, Muslim rule was growing weak in southern Spain. The northern and central parts of Spain were becoming more powerful under the rule of the **Catholic monarchy**.

King Ferdinand and **Queen Isabella** wanted to unite all of Spain under one crown. Their armies began pushing the Muslim leaders out of Spain.

By 1492, the last Islamic city fell, and Spain became one country under the Royal Monarchy.

That was the same year that **Christopher Columbus** discovered America. The king and queen paid for his ships and travel, and he sailed under the flag of Spain.

Spain grew **very rich** because it controlled all the sales of gold, silver, and spices between the Old World (Europe) and the New World (the Americas).

The return of Christopher Columbus

Did you know?
Columbus was trying to find a new sea route to India when he accidentally discovered America!

You've really helped Leonardo finish this historical timetable! He says **mucho gracias**!

Who ruled Spain during these time periods?

700-1492 AD

1492 AD -

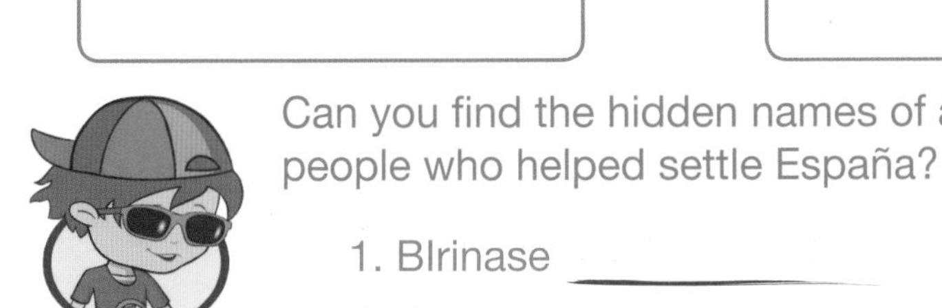

Can you find the hidden names of all the people who helped settle España?

1. Blrinase ____________
2. Kgrese ____________
3. Goviihsts ____________
4. Oroms ____________
5. Marosn ____________

Answers:
1. Iberians;
2. Greeks;
3. Visigoths;
4. Moors;
5. Romans

Answers:
Muslims
(700–1492 AD);
Catholic
Monarchy
(1492 AD –)

Culture and customs

The special traditions of Spain …

Leonardo's been helping us learn about España and the groups that created it. Where people live and what they believe in forms their culture. For example, a farmer or rancher lives on the **land**. Fishermen live by the **ocean**, but a storekeeper lives in a **city** or **town**.
All the different cultures in Spain brought different customs, which they shared with each other.

Language + History + Religion + Culture = CUSTOMS!

So what ties all these people together?

- ✓ Castilian Spanish is spoken by everyone.
- ✓ Most of the Spanish are Catholic (but all religions are accepted).
- ✓ They share certain customs.

Have you heard about fiestas? Flamenco? Bullfighting?
These are three important customs in Spain.

What's a **fiesta**? Fiestas are holidays and giant parties all in one. In Spain, every tiny town and huge city holds fiestas in honor of their patron saint. They all have at least a few fiestas a year. There are parades, huge floats, bands, costumed dancers and singers, food and wine, and a bullfight.

Quizzes! What instrument is played for flamenco music?

guitar

(Hint: You can find the answer on the next page …)

Flamenco and bullfighting ... Oh, my!

Flamenco is a special kind of Spanish **guitar** music and dance. Flamenco comes from long-ago Gypsy music. It tells a story, often about love or a lost loved one. There is usually one dancer and one guitar player ... It's very different from rock bands!

Have you heard about **bullfighting**? Lots of people think it is a sport ... but the Spanish consider it **art**. Bullfighting is a "show"—sort of like an opera. The matador (bullfighter) dances with the wild bull. He uses a small **red capo (cape)** to make the bull follow his spins and turns.

Here's a flamenco dancer and a bullfighter for you to color.

Pleased to meet you ... El Cid

El Cid is Spain's national hero. And he really was a living, breathing person ...

His real name was Rodrigo Díaz de Vivar, but he was called "El Cid," which stands for "outstanding warrior." He was born into a noble family in medieval Spain. The year was either 1040 or 1043—no one is quite sure.

He grew up in the Spanish courts and had the same education as the royal princes of the time. El Cid became a very good military leader.

Did you know?
El Cid fought for both the crown and the Muslims! What makes him a **hero** is that he always fought to unify Spain.

He died in 1099. Since then many poems, songs, stories, plays, and movies have been written about El Cid's bravery and good heart.

Even now, more than 1,000 years later, people talk about El Cid with love. He is a real Spanish hero.

Do you know a famous national hero from your country?

Pleased to meet both of you ...
Don Quixote and Miguel de Cervantes

Have you heard of Miguel de Cervantes? He wrote ***Don Quixote*** (Key-oh-tay). It is one of the most famous books in the world!
Leonardo will tell you a little bit about its adventures ...

The Story of Don Quixote

Don Quixote is a middle-aged gentleman, who comes from the province called La Mancha in central Spain. He believes in the goodness and high ideals he has read about. (And he sees the world a little differently than most people do ...)

"To right the wrongs and defend the poor and helpless; that is my quest."

Don Quixote sets out on **Rocinante**, his old and skinny horse. He is armed with a battered lance (spear) and an aging, rusty sword. He goes off to make the world a better place, and he has some great adventures along the way.

Our hero meets a laborer named **Sancho Panza** and makes him his valet (personal attendant). Along the way, Don Quixote falls in love with **Dulcinea**. She's a peasant woman, but he believes she's a princess. To protect her honor, he fights windmills, believing that "they are bandits waving swords."

Did you know…
Don Quixote is considered the **first modern novel**!
Cervantes was an adventurer in the Spanish Navy. He was captured and held for ransom by pirates! He wrote Don Quixote in the early 1600s, when he was 60 years old.

Do you know a famous writer in your language or from your country? ______________________

Pleased to meet you ...

King of Spain

Spain's King is **Don Felipe VI**. He is the third youngest monarch in the world. Before he became king in 2014, his title was Prince of Asturias.

From the time he was young, Don Felipe was educated and trained to be Spain's King. His parents are King **Don Juan Carlos I** and **Queen Doña Sofia**.

His father brought democracy back to Spain in 1975, after many years of dictatorial* rule. The Spanish were very happy to get their government and freedom back, and they love the Royal Family.

* Dictatorial rule is when someone, usually a military man, takes control of a country. The dictator has total power over everything and everyone.

King Don Felipe VI is married to **Queen Letizia**. She was a TV newswoman before they were married. They have two daughters. **Leonor**, **Princess of Asturias**, is the oldest. She was born in 2005. Her younger sister, Sofía (known as **Infanta Sofía**), was born in 2007.

What does the title "Prince or Princess of Asturias" mean?
It's the title given to the first child born to the Spanish King and Queen. It tells everyone that the child will be the next King or Queen of Spain.

Can you put the right names in each box?

King ____________ & Queen ____________

Daughter ____________

Daughter ____________

Pleased to meet you ... Get to know some super-cool people with ties to Spain!

Sometimes there are **important things and names** that don't make it into history books. This is Leonardo's list of famous people you probably know—but your parents might not. Some of them were born in Spain—others have Spanish ancestors.

Do you know what each of these people is famous for? Draw a line between the person's name and what they do.

Penelope Cruz (born in Spain)	Singer
Shakira (born in Colombia)	Tennis star
Jennifer Lopez (born in Bronx, New York City)	Actress
Eva Longoria (born in Texas, USA)	Actor
Antonio Banderas (born in Spain)	Actress
Javier Bardem (born in Spain)	Soccer star
Lionel Messi (born in Argentina)	Actress
Rafael Nadal (born in Spain)	Actor

Do you like soccer? **Messi** is considered to be one of the **best soccer players ever**! He was born in Argentina, but he lives in Spain and plays for its team. He has won five FIFA Ballons d'Or; eight La Liga titles; four UEFA Champions League tournaments, and four Copas del Rey (King's Cup).

Color Messi's soccer shirt in Spain's colors.

Bon Appetite

Or "buen provecho" in Spanish ...
All about Spanish food and customs

In Spain, eating is an event! It's a chance to chat with friends and family. It doesn't matter whether you are having a big meal or only a tapa. The company is as important as the food.

What time do we eat?

The Spanish people eat at times that may be very different from when you eat at home. **Lunch** is eaten around 2 p.m. (14.00) or 3 p.m. (15.00) in the afternoon. **Dinner** usually begins at 10 p.m. (22.00) at night. This means you get to stay up really, really late!

Tapas keep you from feeling hungry!

Don't worry that you'll starve between meals ... It is **impossible** to be hungry in Spain! That's because people are always stopping for tapas. **Tapas** are like a snack—but better. A tapa is a bite-sized portion of almost anything you want.

Every café has tapas, so you can taste all sorts of things and eat with your fingers! Tapas can be made with meat, ham, fish, eggs, poultry, veggies, cheese, potatoes, meat ... or a mix of more than one. And there are always **las aceitunas** ... that's Spanish for olives.

Quizzes! Can you guess what a **tortilla de patatas** is?

A. Turtle taco **B.** Spinach ice cream **C.** Onion cookie **D.** Potato omelet

Answer: D. Potato omelet

Bon Appetite

Spanish cuisine ... Try some famous dishes

Paella (pay-ee-ay-ya) is a very famous Spanish dish. It's made in a pan big enough to feed 20 or more people. Fresh fish, shrimp, lobster, and perhaps chicken—plus tomatoes, onion, garlic, and the spice called "saffron"—are cooked over a very special rice grown in Valencia. It is the perfect meal to share with friends!

Jamón (hay-mon) is the Spanish word for ham, and it is everywhere. But it's probably nothing like the ham you know. For everyday eating there is Jamón Serrano (ham from the mountains). For special occasions—or just because you like it—there's Jamón Ibérico (Iberian ham from pigs who are fed mainly acorns).

The best breakfast or bedtime snack in the world is **Churros** and **Chocolate Caliente** (hot chocolate). Spanish hot chocolate is almost like pudding. It's thick, creamy, and unimaginably good. Churros are deep-fried ropes of dough. You dunk and swirl them in your chocolate caliente and use them like a spoon.

Gazpacho is a cold soup, usually made with tomatoes, cucumber, bread, garlic, and olive oil. It can also have crushed almonds.

Want to learn a few new words so you can order food in Spanish?

Leonardo wants to help you get ready to order food in Spain! 

You know **niñas** y **niños** (girls and boys) get to stay up really late and eat out with their **madres** y **padres** (mothers and fathers). One reason is because they like the same foods as adults.

So what does everyone eat?

Desayuno (breakfast) is not big.
Café or **zumo de naranja** (orange juice), pan (bread) or pan con tomate (bread with tomato, olive oil, and garlic), or churros y chocolate caliente.

Comida is the word for **lunch** *and* the word for **food**! This is the BIG meal of the day.

- People often order the **Menú del Día** or Special of the Day.
- **Pollo** (chicken)
- **Pescado** (fish)
- **Paella**, **occido**, or **fabada** (types of bean-and-meat stew)
- **Calamares fritos** (fried calamari [squid])
- **Sopa** (soup)
- **Ensalada** (salad)
- And … **fruta** (fruit) for dessert.

Are you still hungry?

And what about dinner?

Cena (dinner) is a smaller meal. Do you remember what time it is eaten? Dinner can be pollo, pescado, **huevos** (eggs), or lots of tapas. Here are some good tapas to choose:

Empanadas
(like a turnover filled with shrimp, jamón, or cheese)

Gambas a la ajillo
(shrimp in garlic sauce)

Croquettes
(like meatballs—filled with cheese, jamón, or meat)

Or you can choose:

- **Queso** (cheese)
- **Patatas** bravas (crisp potatoes in sauce) or huevos
- For veggies, **espárragos** (asparagus) or **pisto** (Spanish ratatouille—a mixture of tomatoes, onions, zucchini, eggplant, and garlic).

Choose your favorite menu for each meal and write it here:

Desayuno ______________________

Comida ______________________

Cena or Tapas ______________________

Can you find and circle the Spanish words for these foods in the word search puzzle?

Tortilla
Jamón
Aceitunas
Paella
Churros
Gazpacho
Café con leche
Pollo
Pescado
Sopa
Ensalada
Fruta
Empanadas
Gambas
Naranja
Espárragos
Huevos

A	P	A	W	W	S	C	C	F	U	A	P	R	P	G
L	E	D	S	K	O	A	E	H	R	J	H	Q	D	Z
L	S	Y	O	K	W	F	D	C	U	U	V	E	O	E
I	C	N	P	Q	R	E	S	A	V	R	T	U	H	T
T	A	S	A	N	F	C	S	A	N	P	R	A	W	E
R	D	O	V	M	S	O	L	K	B	A	U	O	S	V
O	O	V	E	I	D	N	W	H	N	M	P	P	S	D
T	C	E	C	W	A	L	Z	O	L	W	A	M	M	P
F	S	U	S	R	N	E	H	R	X	R	D	G	E	B
G	N	H	A	O	J	C	K	H	R	P	O	L	L	O
S	L	N	M	O	A	H	U	A	L	L	E	A	P	N
D	J	A	B	P	T	E	G	L	H	E	Z	H	L	D
A	J	J	Z	S	P	O	E	N	S	A	L	A	D	A
P	H	A	X	J	S	A	N	U	T	I	E	C	A	Q
J	G	I	G	M	J	B	I	Y	K	Z	V	X	K	O

How do you say it in Spanish?

You've learned to order food on your vacation in España, but what about other words? Understanding Español is easier than you think. Many words sound a lot like they do in English. That's because they come from Latin. There are even English words we use every day that are really Spanish. Mosquito, burro, and adios are three examples.

Being polite and friendly in Spanish ...

English	Spanish
Hello or Hi	**Hola**
Good morning	**Buenos días**
Good afternoon	**Buenas tardes**
Good evening	**Buenas noches**
Please	**Por favor**
Thank you	**Gracias**
You're welcome	**De nada**
How are you?	**¿Cómo está? or ¿Qué tal?**
Then you can say	**Bien, gracias**—This means "I'm good."
Nice to meet you	**Mucho gusto**
Yes / Yes, please	**Si / Si, por favor**
No / No, thanks	**No** (just like English) **/ No, gracias**
I'm sorry / Excuse me	**Perdón / Disculpe**
What is your name?	**¿Como te llaman?**
My name is ...	**Me llamo ...**

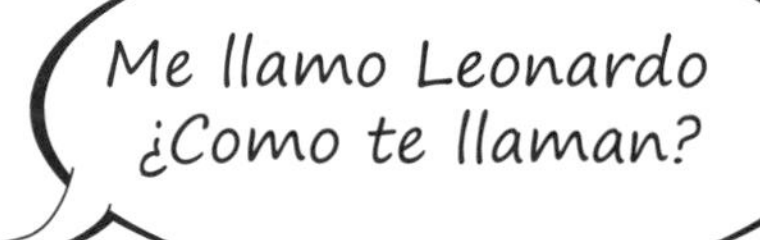

More Spanish words ...

Some really, really important words and phrases to know:

Do you speak English?	**Habla usted inglés, por favor?**
I don't understand.	**No entiendo / ¡No comprendo!**
Please speak slower.	**Por favor habla más despacio.**
Where is the bathroom?	**¿Dónde está el baño?**
Go / Stop	**Adalante / Alto**
Good / Bad	**Bien / Mal**

Did you know?
In Spanish, you put the question mark upside down at the beginning of the question—and right side up at the end! That's so you know it's a question even before you start reading it. Exclamation points are used the same way.

Some fun Spanish slang ...

OK	**¡Vale!**
Cool	**Guay**
Don't worry about it.	**No pasa nada.**
Speak (to me)	**Dígame**

Let's learn to count in Spanish so you can order as many sweets as you want.

Zero	**Cero**
One	**Uno**
Two	**Dos**
Three	**Tres**
Four	**Cuatro**
Five	**Cinco**
Six	**Seis**
Seven	**Siete**
Eight	**Ocho**
Nine	**Nueve**
Ten	**Diez**

Help Leonardo to count ...
Cero
Uno
____
Tres
Cuatro
Cinco
____
Siete
Ocho
____
Diez

Holidays and special days in Spain ...

Just like you, the Spanish people have some holidays they love to celebrate. They might celebrate them a little differently than you do, but that makes it fun.

Merry Christmas

The **Spanish celebrate ¡Feliz Navidad!** (Merry Christmas) for two weeks! **Papa Noel** (Santa) brings presents twice. A few come on Christmas Day, but most of them are given on January 6. That's the day of the Fiesta de Los Tres Reyes Mages (Three Magic Kings).

Happy New Year

Spanish people love to celebrate the **¡Feliz Año Nuevo!** (Happy New Year)! Thousands of people go to Madrid's Puerta del Sol. This square is in the exact center of Madrid. There's a big clock that rings in the New Year with 12 chimes at midnight.

It's a Spanish tradition to eat 12 grapes—one for each of the clock's chimes. It's said that if you get them all eaten before the chimes end, you will have good luck and wealth in the new year.

On your birthday ...
It's your treat! That means **you** make the cake or cupcakes to share with family and friends!

When a child loses a tooth ...
When you lose a tooth in España, a small mouse named **Ratoncito Pérez** comes to get it and leaves you a few coins. Do you want a mouse on your pillow?

What happens in your country when you lose a tooth?

More fun stuff about Spain ...

Everyone needs **vacaciones** ...

that's Spanish for vacation or holiday! Kids get a school break during the summer. And in Spain, even grown-ups get a summer break. August means vacation time. Businesses close and people go on holiday.

During August, Spanish families head to the **playa** (beach) or **montañas** (mountains) for a four-week vacation.

Let's discover majority rule. Check with your family members. How many prefer the **playa** ________ ?
How many prefer the **montañas** ________ ?

Are you interested in outer space?
Did you know a Spaniard **invented the astronaut suit**? In 1935, Emilio Herrera Linares, a physicist and military engineer from Granada, invented and built the first model of an astronaut suit.

Do you use a stapler from time to time?
The next time you use a stapler, say **gracias**. In the 18th century, a Spaniard made the first stapler for Louis XV, the French King. **Every single staple was engraved with the royal emblem!**

Did you know?
There are **five main languages** spoken in Spain. That's because the tribes who settled in Spain long ago brought their own languages. The areas they settled gradually became separate kingdoms—which are Spain's provinces today.

Castilian Spanish is spoken by everyone, but Spaniards also speak the language of their province. In addition, many Spaniards speak a foreign language—especially English or Arabic.

Spain **is famous for ...**

Art and Museums

El Prado is called Madrid's "Museum of Masterpieces," because it is home to a huge number of paintings by many of Spain's greatest artists—**Goya**, **Velázquez**, and **El Greco**.

Reina Sofia (officially called **Museo Nacional Centro de Arte Reina Sofía**) is second only to the Prado in international importance and fame. **Pablo Picasso** is the star! His painting "**Guernica**" is Spain's national treasure. It's often called the most important painting of the 20th century.

Did you know?
Picasso drew a picture of a **white dove** and used it as a symbol to help end war. His dove is the **international symbol of peace**.

In Bilbao, the **Guggenheim Museum**, or **El Goog** as residents call it, is world famous—and it helped give new life to the entire city. El Goog even has its own mascot—a **puppy** that's more than 12 meters high (over 40 feet). The puppy is covered in flowers all year!

Trivia time: What do you know about Spain?

1. On what continent is Spain located? ______________

2. What two countries make up the Iberian Peninsula? ______________

   ____

3. What other country is Spain's neighbor? ______________

4. What is the name of the sea on one side of Spain? ______________

5. What colors are on the Spanish flag? ______________ ______________

6. What is the insignia on the Spanish flag? ______________

7. What is the capital city of Spain? ______________

8. What type of money does Spain use? ______________

9. What is the name of Spain's national hero? ______________

10. What was the name of the man who fought windmills in a very famous book?

    ____

11. What special kind of food do the Spanish people snack on all day?

    ____

12. Which snack was your favorite? ______________

Answers: 1. Europe; 2. Spain and Portugal; 3. France/Andorra; 4. Mediterranean Sea; 5. Red and Yellow; 6. Spain's Coat of Arms; 7. Madrid; 8. Euro; 9. El Cid; 10. Don Quixote; 11. Tapas

Now some super-tough trivia to test your brainpower.

1. Which one of these is the special symbol for Madrid:

Trevi Fountain   Pagoda   El Oso y El Madrono   Brooklyn Bridge

2. Circle the city where the famous architect Gaudi worked:

Madrid   Seville   Barcelona   Granada   Valencia   Cadiz

3. Can you name the one thing Gaudí never, ever used in his buildings?

____

4. Can you name the Spanish city that was once famous for being the center of education and culture for all of Europe?

____

5. Here is a map of Spain, but all the cities have been deleted. Can you help Leonardo find Spain's major cities?

Hint: You can look back to page 12 if you need help.

6. What makes Spain's national anthem different from yours and almost any national anthem? ______________________________

Answers:
1. El Oso y El Madrono; 2. Barcelona; 3. A straight line; 4. Seville;
6. Spain's national anthem has no words.

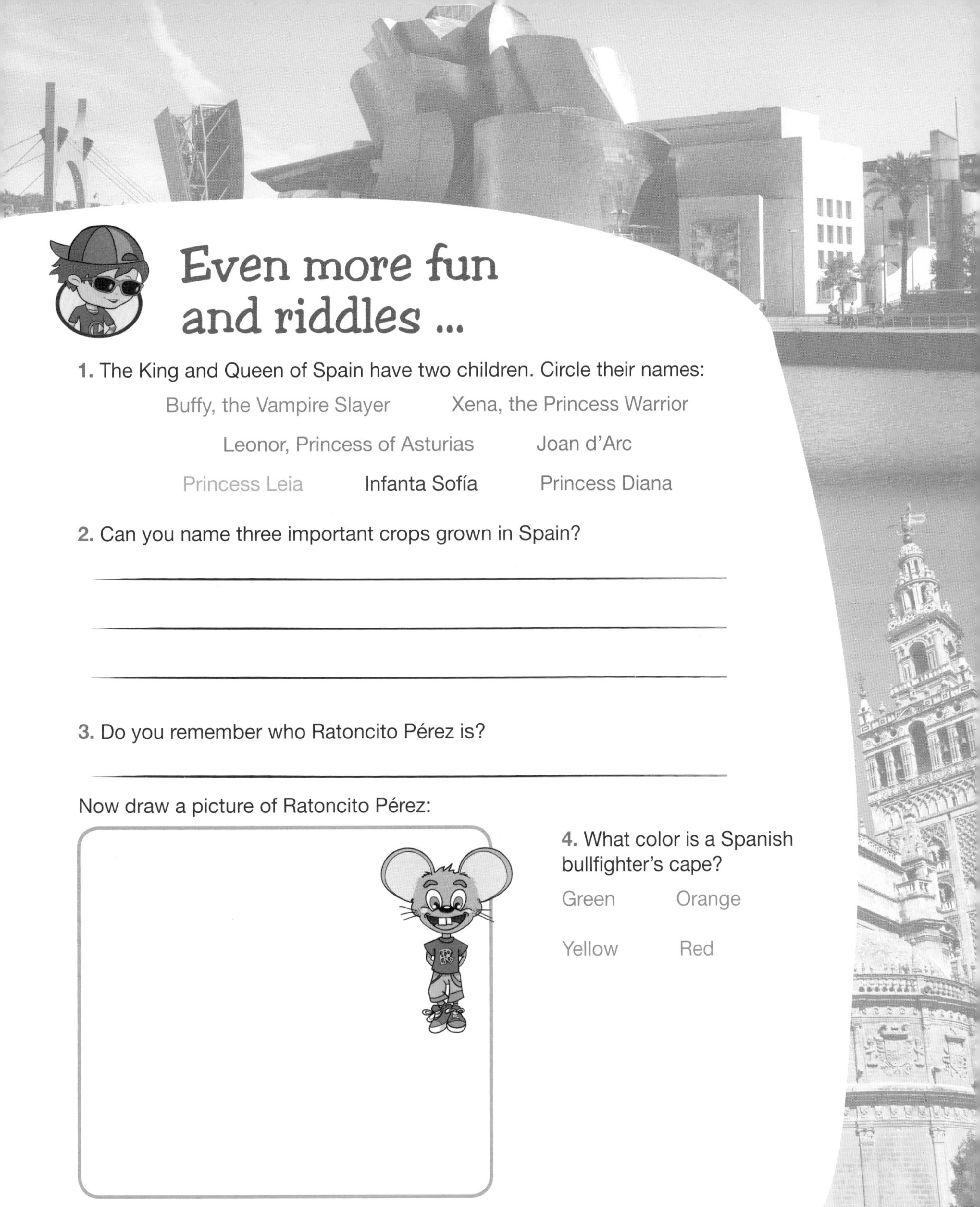

Even more fun and riddles ...

1. The King and Queen of Spain have two children. Circle their names:

Buffy, the Vampire Slayer Xena, the Princess Warrior

Leonor, Princess of Asturias Joan d'Arc

Princess Leia Infanta Sofía Princess Diana

2. Can you name three important crops grown in Spain?

____

____

____

3. Do you remember who Ratoncito Pérez is?

____

Now draw a picture of Ratoncito Pérez:

4. What color is a Spanish bullfighter's cape?

Green Orange

Yellow Red

Answers:
1. Leonor, Princess of Asturias, and Infanta Sofía; 2. Olive trees, grapes for wine, almond trees, or tomatoes; 3. The Tooth Fairy—but he is a mouse! 4. Red

And to sum it all up ...

SUMMARY OF THE TRIP

We had great fun! What a pity it is over ...

Which places did we visit?

____

____

Whom did we meet ...

- Did you meet tourists from other countries? yes / no
  If you did meet tourists, where did they come from?
  (Name their nationalities):

____

Shopping and souvenirs ...

- What did you buy on the trip?

____

____

- What did you want to buy, but ended up not buying?

____

Experiences

- What are the most memorable experiences of the trip?

____

____

____

What was each family member's favorite place?

_______________ : ____________________________

_______________ : ____________________________

_______________ : ____________________________

_______________ : ____________________________

Grade the most beautiful places and the best experiences of your journey:

First place

Second place

Third place

And now, a difficult task—talk with your family and decide:

What did everyone enjoy most on the trip?

Date	What did we do?

A journal

Date	What did we do?

ENJOY MORE FUN ADVENTURES WITH LEONARDO AND FlyingKids

ITALY

KIDS' TRAVEL GUIDE ROME

THAILAND

KIDS' TRAVEL GUIDE thailand & bangkok

JAPAN

FRANCE

GERMANY

SPAIN

AUSTRALIA

USA

KIDS' TRAVEL GUIDE SAN DIEGO

SPECIAL EDITIONS

UNITED KINGDOM

AGES 4-8

FOR FREE DOWNLOADS OF MORE ACTIVITIES, GO TO WWW.THEFLYINGKIDS.COM